pocket posh® tips for quilters

Jodie Davis
and
Jayne Davis

**Andrews McMeel
Publishing, LLC**

Kansas City • Sydney • London

POCKET POSH® TIPS FOR QUILTERS

copyright © 2011 by Jodie Davis and Jayne Davis. All rights
reserved. Printed in China. No part of this book may be used or
reproduced in any manner whatsoever without written permission
except in the case of reprints in the context of reviews.

Andrews McMeel Publishing, LLC
an Andrews McMeel Universal company
1130 Walnut Street, Kansas City, Missouri 64106

www.andrewsmcmeel.com

11 12 13 14 15 SHZ 10 9 8 7 6 5 4 3 2 1

ISBN: 978-1-4494-0342-3

Library of Congress Control Number: 2010937877

Hand drawings by Iia Owens-Williams
Quilt and Fabric design by Erin McMorris

ATTENTION: SCHOOLS AND BUSINESSES
Andrews McMeel books are available at quantity discounts with
bulk purchase for educational, business, or sales promotional use.
For information, please e-mail the Andrews McMeel Publishing
Special Sales Department:
specialsales@amuniversal.com

contents

acknowledgments

When we started mulling about how to round up a collection of tips for quilters, we decided to go right to the source. Thus many, many e-mails went out to quilt shop owners, designers, and industry leaders asking for their favorite tips. A huge "Thank You" to each and every one who responded. We couldn't have done it without you. Special thanks go to the members of the Gold Coast Quilters Guild of Boca Raton, Florida, for sharing their quilting tip collection. We've also added tips gleaned from our two lifetimes of quilting.

introduction

Wikipedia tells us that quilting is the stitching together of layers of padding and fabric and that it may date back to ancient Egypt. In the past quilting was a product of necessity to patch clothing and make it warmer, and to make quilts to warm beds.

Today we quilt for the sheer joy of it and as an outlet for our creativity. Our quilting ranges from the very traditional to the most avant-garde. Anything goes, and the colors sing, whether muted or brilliant. Many quilters embrace the latest technology, while others savor quilting by hand and others enjoy the full gamut.

We're thankful to be part of this passionate and diverse worldwide community of quilters and know you are thankful, too. We hope you enjoy this collection and discover some tips that will give you an "aha" moment, making your quilting faster or easier and always more fun.

Jodie and Jayne

let's get organized

let's get organized

May your bobbins always be full.
—*Anonymous*

With everyone having a cell phone nowadays, I keep a list of all my books and patterns in my phone so if I am out and about I can check my phone to see whether I have already purchased it. I have been known to have three or more copies of the same pattern. Thank goodness for cell phones; you can also store a list of fabrics you are searching for.

Material Girls Quilts

thematerialgirlsquilting.com

When you have a whole day or half a day to quilt, spend it designing and cutting. Organize the pieces on your design wall, in plastic bags or containers, or on paper plates that you can stack. Discipline yourself to keep designing and cutting all day. Don't sew! Then, later in the week when you only have minutes to sew, you are ready! A side benefit of spending the day designing is that you may find there is something that is just not working when you view the pieces on your design wall. It is much easier to make changes before they are sewn.

Debbie Caffrey

Debbiescreativemoments.com

Hold everything in place: Cut a piece of Rubbermaid drawer liner into a small rectangle or square. Place the liner piece beside your sewing machine to keep scissors, stiletto, and other tools handy. They won't roll off the table when you sew. These pieces of drawer liner can hold foot pedals steady on tile or wooden floors. You can put a large piece under your sewing machine so it doesn't move or under a portable ironing surface to prevent the board from sliding while in use.

Gold Coast Quilters Guild

Keeping your thimble in place: Lick your finger before putting on your thimble. This will stop it from slipping.

Gold Coast Quilters Guild

Organizing rotary cutting rulers: Where do you put rulers so they are accessible but out of the way? Each ruler has a small hole, but it's too small to put on a hook. Thread flat ribbon through the hole and make a loop, then hang the ruler from a set of hooks. It's neat against the wall, not taking up any table space, it's easy to find, and the flat ribbon doesn't interfere with the ruler's sitting flat on the fabric.

Gold Coast Quilters Guild

Store your quilts in pillowcases or fabric bags, which allow them to breathe. Never store quilts in plastic bags.

Labeling your ruler: Use address labels on all your plastic rulers so you don't lose them.

Gold Coast Quilters Guild

I use the little sticky hangers that are removable. I stick them on a storage door at the shop so that we always have different size rulers without anyone walking away with our own personal rulers. I also use them in my sewing room. I keep all my rulers on the back of my door, and then I always know where they are. We have an abundance of sticky hangers. Love them!

Material Girls Quilts
thematerialgirlsquilting.com

Containers for small projects: In grocery stores, some vegetables are sold in small Styrofoam containers. These containers are good for storing small projects like the block of the month and for keeping larger scraps together from projects you are working on. You can also stick pins in them as you are working. They stack nicely and come in lots of sizes.

Gold Coast Quilters Guild

Styrofoam containers: Stack one or two Styrofoam trays beside your sewing machine to hold scissors, bobbins, and so on. Line everything up in the tray or on the bed of the machine the same way every time and you can reach, without looking, for just the right tool. You can stand your stiletto and seam ripper upright through the side of the foam tray. No more poked fingers, and they are always handy.

Gold Coast Quilters Guild

If your quilts are stored folded, take them out and refold from time to time. Be sure to change the folding pattern.

Storing accessories for appliqué and hand piecing: Keep all accessories for appliqué and hand piecing in a worm binder. These are normally used by fishermen to organize their fishing lures. It has a number of thick plastic sleeves that keep everything organized and a hard shell that folds out to be a stable surface when you are traveling. It is indispensable for quilting and can also be used to store knitting needles by size. They come in all sizes from small to jumbo.

Gold Coast Quilters Guild

To store your quilts, roll them on cardboard tubes covered with acid-free tissue paper. Cover the quilt with acid-free tissue paper, too. Tubes from wrapping paper are often the right size for small quilts.

Keeping extension cords under control: To keep your extension cords organized between uses, bundle them with a covered elastic ponytail band. These can be purchased in the hair goods aisle at drugstores.

Gold Coast Quilters Guild

To keep quilting kits and projects organized, condensed, and all in one place: Put quilting kits or projects, along with fabrics, special notions, directions, and so on selected for the project on top of a piece of cardboard and place in a food sealer bag. Using a vacuum sealer, extract the air out of the food sealer bag. The cardboard will help support the package for storage in an upright position. These bags can be stored in a drawer or file cabinet and will not take up much space. You can also make a label and place it on the cardboard to identify the kit or project. These project bags are safe and airtight. They protect your fabric and other items in the bag from humidity, bugs, and dust. Having all your projects in one place may inspire you to work on them. And having your fabrics for each project together and labeled means that you won't accidentally use the fabric intended for that project for something else.

Gold Coast Quilters Guild

it's all about the fabric

it's all about the fabric

I'm a material girl. Want to see
my fabric collection?
—Anonymous

Take fat quarters of the fabrics and lay them on top of each other, allowing about an inch strip to show. This will give you a better idea of how they will blend in a quilt rather than looking at whole bolts next to each other; that's way too much fabric to compare for small piecing. When you decide which colors and prints you like, purchase the necessary amounts of fabric. This also allows you to throw in a piece to make the quilt pop and see what a wild color will do for you.

Debbie Deen
Formerly Quilt Shop of Anderson
Anderson, South Carolina

Look for fabrics with color combinations that are either across from each other on the color wheel or close neighbors. You can then vary the hues and values within these color choices (Fig. 1).

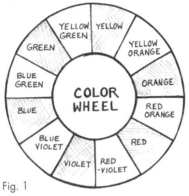

YELLOW GREEN | YELLOW
GREEN | YELLOW ORANGE
BLUE GREEN | ORANGE
BLUE | **COLOR WHEEL** | RED ORANGE
BLUE VIOLET | RED
VIOLET | RED -VIOLET

Fig. 1

I'm a pack rat. A professional organizer helped me get my quilting stuff under control. The answer? Get a calendar and write down what you expect to do in quilts for 2 years. Shop from home and kit all projects. Get rid of everything else. So I did. And so can you.

Mark Lipinski
Pickle Road Studios
marklipinski.com

Deciding on a border for your quilt: When you cannot decide which fabrics to use for borders, hang or clothespin the quilt top on a drapery rod. Fold border choices to approximate size and pin to the edge of the quilt. Look at the choices in the evening and then in the daytime. Some will jump out as horrid and others will jump out as perfect. The lighting makes a big difference.

Gold Coast Quilters Guild

Here's a tip for shop owners and quilters when selling or purchasing extra-wide backing fabric: As hard as they try, fabric distributors never wind the extra-wide backing on the bolt correctly; it is always crooked. Once they receive the wide backings, shop owners should cut 1 or 2 inches along the selvage at the end of the bolt and tear the strip across the entire width of the fabric. You now have a straight edge to measure from; if a customer wants 3 yards, measure out your 3 yards, make a cut in the selvage, and tear again across the width of the fabric. Customers, especially if buying from a discount store, should request that the fabric be torn rather than cut with either a scissors or a rotary cutter. I have had many customers bring me an extra-wide backing that, once unfolded, looks like a parallelogram and does not fit the dimensions of their quilt.

Barb Hoekstra
Ashland Area Fabric & Quilt Company
ashlandquilt.com

I am very fond of using starch when I quilt. It helps keep the grain of the fabric square and also helps prevent premature fraying. Starched pieces are much easier to match corners, for instance. I also prewash my fabrics in a pillowcase to help prevent fraying.

Bolt Neighborhood Fabric Boutique
boltfabricboutique.com

We make T-shirt quilts and memory quilts as our business. Here are a few tips that are specific to using clothing in quilts:

- When preparing shirts for a T-shirt quilt, avoid using fabric softener in the washer or dryer sheets in the dryer, as they can affect the bond of the fusible interfacing to T-shirt.
- Always cut the T-shirt block to be used 3 or 4 inches larger around the image or design you are planning to use. Fuse your interfacing to the shirt and then recut to the exact measurements of the intended block size.
- When choosing clothing to use in a memory quilt, consider washability, potential shrinkage (wool), possible dye transfer (silk ties or never-worn clothing), and raveling. After making hundreds of memory quilts, I now refuse to use leather, knit sweaters, and socks. These are not good items to include in a memory quilt.

- Tie quilts can be stunning and a great way to showcase beautiful tie collections. Ties should always be prewashed by soaking in warm water and a dye fixative such as Retayne. Lay them flat to dry before using them in a quilt.

- When choosing a pattern for a quilt to be made with clothing, consider the thicknesses of the fabrics to be used. If you are using denim, for example, it will be difficult to achieve sharp points, so a mariner's compass pattern would be a regrettable choice.

- If you're working with sheer, silky, or thin fabrics, it's useful to add a lightweight fusible interfacing to the back in order to stabilize the fabric and make it easier to use.

Tina Schwager and Julianne Walther
Patchwork Memories, Inc.
Creating Quilts That Celebrate Life
patchworkmemories.com

Choose a very busy print fabric backing for longarm quilting when you're just starting out. This way, you will not be discouraged when you see all your start and stops on the back when changing thread colors.

Pam Clarke
Home Stitches/Lines with Designs
homestitches.com

17

I do love to mix different textiles, scales, and mediums if the color and patterns relate. I am always looking for harmony in imperfect juxtapositions. Mixtures bring life to the color schemes.

Kaffe Fassett
Kaffe Fassett Design
kaffefassett.com

Using fabric for a specific quilt: If you buy fabric for a certain quilt pattern but cannot find all the fabrics necessary to start the quilt, put the pattern and the fabrics you have already in a basket or container. Then, when you find the remainder of the fabrics, you have not cut into any of the fabrics already designated for that pattern.

Gold Coast Quilters Guild

Measure and then fold fabric for your stash. Place a piece of painter's tape on the top corner and mark it with the yardage. This way, you won't have to keep unfolding fabric to find one with the needed yardage for a specific project.

Fabric shopping: When shopping for material for a project, pin together small samples of fabric already assembled from that project and keep in your purse. When you find more material, attach samples to the same pin. This way, you always have samples with you when you come across fabric that might fit with your project. You might think you remember that shade of blue, but when you get home it is nothing like you thought. If you had your samples with you, you would have known it wasn't right.

Gold Coast Quilters Guild

To wash or not to wash: This is an ongoing question for quilters, and most agree it depends on how the finished piece will be used. If it's a wall hanging that will probably never be washed, there's no reason to prewash. If it's placemats or a baby quilt that will be washed frequently, prewash the fabric. Hand quilters generally prefer to work on prewashed fabric because it "needles" better. If the fabrics have not been prewashed, the finished piece will shrink a bit when washed, resulting in a slight puckering. Many people prefer this look, but if this isn't how you want your finished piece to look after washing, prewash the fabrics.

Bleeding: This is another reason to prewash fabrics, especially very dark colors and reds. A good test is to toss a scrap of muslin into the wash water with each fabric. The muslin scrap will absorb any bleeding color, and you'll know in a flash whether the fabric is colorfast.

Home remedies added to the wash water might keep some fabrics from bleeding, but they certainly are not guaranteed. Vinegar, iodized salt, and Epsom salts can be tried. The best way is to keep rinsing the fabric until the rinse water runs clear.

Choosing fabric: When you're considering fabrics to buy, take a few steps back and look at the fabrics again. They can look very different from this view.

Take your fabric selections to a window, or better yet, go outside. Artificial light can mask the true colors.

What's the number one rule in selecting fabrics? There are no rules! Choose what pleases you. Be fearless! Tried and true is fine, but why not try something a bit different? You'll love it.

Who is your best friend in selecting fabrics? Well, your local quilt shop, of course.

tools of the trade

tools of the trade

Quilters never grow old. They just go to pieces.
—Anonymous

To prevent unauthorized users from dulling your fabric cutting shears, use a padlock on the handles. Actually, a combination or key lock will do. Stash the combination or the key deep in your sewing box or machine cabinet drawer. No family member will look that far. This tip came from a viewer of our television show.

Marianne Fons
Co-host, Love of Quilting

I don't have a lot of tools, but I do splurge on scissors. I have a pair strictly for fabric, one for fusible web (Teflon coated), and one for anything else, fabric or paper.

Linda Lum DeBono
lindalumdebono.com

When using your ruler, always place your little finger on the noncutting side. It will do two things: hold the ruler more firmly and keep your finger away from the blade.

Janet Kugler
Quilter's Delight
quiltersdelight-nebraska.blogspot.cpm

Don't toss your dull and nicked rotary cutter blades. Instead, use them on a second rotary cutter for cutting paper, gift wrap, or wallpaper. The blades still have lots of useful life in them and work great.

Mary Miller
The Quilt Block
iowaquiltblock.com

I like to keep thread snips by my machine and not scissors. It takes more time to put your fingers through the handle holes in scissors than it does to pick up snips to cut thread.

Don't use big scissors near your machine. They bang into your machine and mark it up.

Sharon Rehrig
Teacher & Retreats
timelystitches.com

. . . .

Rotary blade getting dull? Crumple a piece of aluminum foil, lay it on your cutting mat, and cut through the foil several times.

Ann Taylor
Buttonwood Quilts
buttonwoodquilts.com

. . . .

Portable pressing surface: Don't you just hate to wait during a workshop to use the ironing board? Never wait again! Make a lightweight, portable ironing surface to keep next to your sewing machine, right at your work station. It's simple and inexpensive. Go to a home improvement store and buy a flame-resistant ceiling tile. Cover with two layers of batting and one layer of cotton duck or heavyweight poplin. Make the duck layer a little bigger than the batting layers. Glue the duck to the back of the ceiling tile and allow to dry overnight. There you go! Your very own portable pressing surface.

Gold Coast Quilters Guild

Portable pressing table: Purchase a wooden folding snack table. These are very reasonably priced and can be found in Target and Wal-Mart. These tables don't take up a lot of room and can be placed beside your chair. A small ironing surface and travel iron fit nicely on top of the snack table. It's great for classes and workshops and eliminates jumping up and down from the sewing machine to the ironing board.

Gold Coast Quilters Guild

Cleaning a dirty iron: When your iron gets dirty, try ironing over a damp Mr. Clean Magic Eraser and it's clean again. Fold a kitchen towel under the Magic Eraser so the ironing surface doesn't get wet. This spongy thing cleans everything! Great for stubborn dirt or sticky labels or residue on anything.

Gold Coast Quilters Guild

If the iron is really a mess, set it face down in a shallow baking pan or jelly roll pan. Add ¼ inch of white vinegar and leave the iron to soak a few minutes (Fig. 2). Wipe dry.

Fig. 2

More iron cleaning tips: To clean the sole plate of your iron when it gets gunked up without having to wait for it to cool down, pour table salt in a line about 1 by 6 inches on a terry towel. Move your iron back and forth over the salt and voilà! All the residue comes right off.

Gold Coast Quilters Guild

Portable small design wall: Four 1-inch-diameter PVC pipes cut into 4-foot sections and four PVC elbows (found at Home Depot or Lowe's) can be put together to form a square. Cut a piece of white flannel to size and hem. Add a 1½-inch-wide sleeve on all four sides, 1 inch in from each end. Slide each PVC pipe section into a sleeve, and then connect the pipes together with the PVC elbows. This can be put together in a snap and used in classes, workshops, or smaller sewing areas as a design wall. After you use it, you can easily take it apart and store it.

Gold Coast Quilters Guild

Needle sorter tip: Purchase an inexpensive tomato pincushion. They usually are marked off in wedges by green string dividers. Using a fine-point pen, such as a Micron Pigma or Sharpie Ultra-Fine, mark each section with a different needle size. You will always know which size needle you are using when it's missing from your tomato, and you'll have a place to return it to when you need to change. As an extra bonus, buying the type of tomato that comes with the attached strawberry emery and giving your needles a few strokes through the emery before use will tame any burrs and ensure a longer life for your needles.

Gold Coast Quilters Guild

Light boxes are the best way to transfer designs from paper to fabric or paper to fusible webbing. If you have a glass-topped table it's easy to set up a makeshift light box. Buy a fluorescent light fixture used for under-cabinet lighting. Sit at your table and place the light in your lap. Works perfectly.

Plastic templates: To prevent plastic templates from slipping when you are tracing around them, use a little piece of double-stick tape on the back. Your template will lay flat for tracing and not slip on your fabric but will come up easily. Replace the tape when it's not sticking anymore.

Gold Coast Quilters Guild

Putting your walking foot on your machine: If you are having trouble putting your walking foot on your machine, try lowering the feed dogs. This fraction of an inch will help tremendously. Remember to raise them afterward.

Gold Coast Quilters Guild

Another walking foot tip: Sometimes when you put on your walking foot, it seems that you cannot raise the presser foot high enough. Use your knee lift, and it will give you a little more space, enough to put on your walking foot with ease.

Gold Coast Quilters Guild

Extending the life of a rotary cutting blade: When your rotary cutting blade begins to get dull, turn it over. This will give you some more cutting time per blade. This is very handy if you are taking a class and don't have an extra blade with you.

Gold Coast Quilters Guild

Another way to use the seam ripper: Place the handle end of a seam ripper inside a regular-size spool of thread. After chain piecing, place the chain in the ripper and pull down on both sides.

Gold Coast Quilters Guild

Preventing pins from rusting: To keep pins from rusting, take one of those small paper desiccant packs that come in many medications and put it in your pin box. This keeps them smooth and free from rust for years. You can also use the little packets that come in shoe boxes. They also work well in a baggie with water-soluble thread to keep it dry.

Gold Coast Quilters Guild

Machine needle sorter: Take a 6-inch square piece of batting and two 6-inch square pieces of muslin and sandwich them together. Sew the sandwich together all around the sides with half-inch seam. Trim with pinking shears. Draw on the top piece of muslin with a permanent pen, Pigma pen, or very fine Sharpie, marking the square in half horizontally and vertically and then drawing diagonal lines from corner to corner. Mark each of these sections with sizes of machine needles and place the appropriate needles in each section. When you remove a needle from the needle sorter, put a pin in that spot. When you are finished sewing with that needle, you can put it back in its spot. If you sew a piece of ribbon on the corner of this needle sorter, you can attach it to your sewing machine, and your needles will always be handy.

Gold Coast Quilters Guild

. . . .

Cutting accurately: Always roll the rotary cutter away from you. For a crisp cut, use even pressure and start rolling before you reach the fabric and continue after it. You may need to stop cutting halfway through to reposition your hand on the ruler. And get in the habit of closing your rotary cutter before putting it down, or purchase the type with a self-retracting blade.

The object in rotary cutting is to make straight, even cuts as close to the fabric grain as possible. This way, squares and rectangles are cut on the lengthwise and crosswise grain, ensuring that they will not distort as they would if cut with bias edges. You will need a rotary cutter, a cutting mat, and a 6 by 24-inch clear ruler and a 12-inch square clear ruler.

1.   On the cutting mat, fold the fabric in half lengthwise, aligning the selvage edges, with the raw edges to your right and left and the fold closest to you (Fig. 3).

2.   Place the square ruler along the folded edge, making sure it is aligned with the fold. Place the 6 by 24-inch ruler next to the square ruler, butting the edges and having the

long side of the ruler cover the uneven raw edges of the fabric (Fig. 4).

3. Remove the square ruler and make a clean cut along the edge of the long ruler (Fig. 5).

Fig. 3

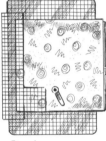

Fig. 4

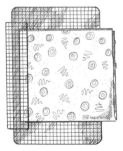

Fig. 5

How a sewing machine stitch is formed: A stitch begins when the needle penetrates the fabric and descends to its lowest point. The bobbin hook then slides by the needle's scarf (the indentation at the back of the needle), catching the upper thread, and carries it around the bobbin and bobbin thread (Fig. 6). The thread is then pulled up into the fabric, completing the stitch (Fig. 7).

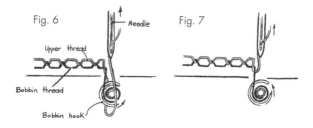

Fig. 6 — Needle, Upper thread, Bobbin thread, Bobbin hook

Fig. 7

Choosing the right sewing machine needle for the job at hand is important. Determine needle size by fabric weight. A 70/10 (70 is the European size and 10 is the American size) or 80/12 works for most quilting fabrics. A 90/14 is best if your quilt sandwich is thick. The universal needle is the one used for most sewing. The thread should pass easily through the eye of the needle. There are special needles for sewing with decorative metallic threads and quilting needles with a special tapered shaft to prevent damaging fabrics when stitching multiple layers. It's important to change your needle after every 8 to 10 hours of sewing for optimum results.

some really good ideas

some really good ideas

When life throws you scraps, make a quilt.
—*Anonymous*

As co-host of Fons & Porter's *Love of Quilting* on public television for many years, I've had the opportunity to share lots of great viewer tips on the air. Liz Porter and I have read hundreds, maybe thousands, of terrific tips at the famous Tip Table, and now my daughter Mary Fons, who's co-hosting with me, shares them at the end of each episode.

We continue to be impressed with the quality, originality, and sense of humor reflected in the tips viewers send. We encourage viewers to send in not only their tip but also any prop or photo we can use to help get their tip across on camera. The lumpy, bumpy packages that arrive in our editorial offices in Winterset, Iowa, are much appreciated. Here's a tip that really works.

Reposition your ironing board so that the narrow, pointed end is to your right (if you are right handed, or vice versa if you are left handed). The standard ironing board is shaped for pressing clothing. We quilters constantly press patchwork units, patchwork blocks, strips of blocks, quilt tops, and backings, all of which are generally square.

By positioning your ironing board so that the wider, square end is right in front of you, you'll have a much handier work space, and the skinny end is an adequate location for your iron. If anyone in the household has a garment that needs pressing, the ironing board is easily repositioned for that person's use.

Marianne Fons
Co-host, Love of Quilting

My tip is the saggy bottom rule. It is for machine sewing two pieces together that are supposed to be the same length but aren't. Place the longer piece on the bottom and the shorter on the top. Match beginning and end and pin each. The extra length is in the middle. The machine feed dogs will help match the two fabrics by feeding a little more of the bottom than the top.

Mill House Quilts
millhousequilts.com

When beginning a quilt project, do this first. Make the binding, press, and roll onto a toilet paper core. Design and print the label and make the sleeve. Put these into a bag with the project, and you have everything ready to finish the project. No more unfinished objects.

Gold Coast Quilters Guild

. . . .

We use masking tape for numbering our blocks and rows. It helps when sewing blocks and rows correctly and also keeps the correct orientation.

Rita Smith
Quiltsmiths
Quiltsmiths.com

. . . .

You are never too experienced to take a class. I have had the pleasure of taking three workshops: fabric dyeing with Donna Barnitz; drafting with Gail Garber, based on her new book, *Flying Colors*; and design explorations with Katie Pasquini Masopust. All of these classes pushed me beyond my groove. Expand your creativity and skills. It is exciting.

Debbie Caffrey
debbiescreativemoments.com

My favorite tip is about rotary cutting. If you always remember to keep the excess fabric out toward your cutting hand, you will save yourself many steps, no longer needing to walk around the table; this works for left or right handers.

Sylvia Dorney
Greenbaum's Quilted Forest
quiltedforest.com

Sew longer and have better posture by placing two doorstops under the back of your machine to raise it 1 inch. You will be amazed at how much easier it is to work on your projects.

Jenice Belling
The Quilted Garden and
Quilted Garden Designs
quiltedgarden.com

Cotton fabric, cotton thread; polyester fabric, polyester thread. Change your needle after every project. Buy the best thread you can afford.

If your rotary cutter leaves fabric behind in the grooves of the cutting mat, it's time to change the blade.

Steve (machine repair)
Quilter's Harvest Shop
quiltersharvestshop.com

Paper cutters are handy for cutting templates, and they leave smooth edges (Fig. 8). For a perfect right angle, line up one side of the template against an inch line on the cutter and cut on your marked line.

Fig. 8

To take cat hair or any hair off a quilt, use a rubber glove. (This also works on furniture.)

Sharon Rehrig
Teacher and Retreats
Timely Stitches
timelystitches@rcn.com

Have sleeves at the ready by making a roll of continuous sleeves. Here's how. From 2 yards of muslin, cut strips 8

inches wide vertically. Seam the strips together into one long strip. Press the seams open. Topstitch from the back side as close to the raw edges as possible (Fig. 9). Press seams again. Press the sleeve in half lengthwise, wrong sides

Fig. 9

together. Roll up. Whenever you need a sleeve, cut off the length you need and finish the ends. You're ready to go.

Gold Coast Quilters Guild

. . . .

Use a medium or fine-grit sandpaper to cut templates. The template will stay in place when you are marking.

· *Ann Taylor*
Buttonwood Quilts
buttonwoodquilts.com

. . . .

Snippets of thread on the floor: When you are piecing, your floor can get covered with all the snipped threads, and then they get tracked all over the house. To eliminate this, take a piece of strapping tape, masking tape, or clear wide tape about 12 inches long. Make a big circle (loop) out of it by joining it to itself, sticky side out. Press the join up under the front right or left side of your sewing table. When you snip some thread, just touch the thread onto the taped surface, and it will stick. Replace your tape when full. No more threads to track around the house or get stuck in your vacuum's beater bar.

Gold Coast Quilters Guild

To make it easier to write on fabric being used for friendship and signature quilts, stabilize the fabric by pressing the shiny side of a piece of freezer paper to the fabric block. After the ink dries, peel off the freezer paper.

Stray threads on your quilt: A comb run across the stitching catches where all the "bridges" are so they can be cleaned off.

Gold Coast Quilters Guild

To transfer designs from a pattern, lay a piece of tulle netting over the design and trace with a permanent marker. Then position the netting on your fabric or quilt, pin in place, and trace the design through the netting using your favorite marking tool.

Removing a drop of blood from your quilt: When you stick yourself with a pin or needle and you get a drop of blood on your quilt, you can remove the blood with your own saliva.

Gold Coast Quilters Guild

Threading a needle: We usually wet the end of our thread before trying to thread a needle. Try wetting the eye of the needle instead. Lick it; it makes threading the needle easier. Also, needle eyes are punched in by machine, and thread will always go through the eye easier from the side the eye was made. So if you having a hard time threading a needle, turn the needle around and try threading from the other side.

Gold Coast Quilters Guild

Seeing the eye of the sewing machine needle: If you have trouble threading the sewing machine needle, put some dark paper or felt in back of the needle, and then you can see the hole.

Gold Coast Quilters Guild

Faux serging: If you do not have a serger and would like to achieve the look, there is a way. Using the blanket stitch on your machine, set the length to very short and the width to very long. The straight stitch should be on the inside (left), with the side stitch going slightly off the fabric (or to the very edge into thin air). This will give you a nice serged look on heavier or stiffer fabric. Thinner fabric will start to roll and give a slightly messy rolled hem look. This is great for the inside of pillowcases.

Gold Coast Quilters Guild

Bobbins matching spools of thread: Fill a bobbin with the same color thread as your spool of thread. Use a golf tee and keep them together. Put the pointed end of the golf tee through the large hole in the bobbin and then slip the point

of the golf tee into the top of the spool of thread (Fig. 10). To keep the bobbin thread from unraveling, cut apart the rings from a black spiral binder. Secure the little rings around the filled bobbins. Everything is neat and tidy, and when you are ready to sew with a certain thread color, you don't waste time filling a bobbin.

Gold Coast Quilters Guild

Fig. 10

Cleaning rotary cutting mats: When your rotary cutting mat gets clogged with fabric threads, cleaning is simple. The next time you buy a new puff for your shower, save the old one. Keep it by your cutting table. Just wipe the mat with it (dry only), and it will easily remove all the lint and debris.

Gold Coast Quilters Guild

Removing threads, lint, and fabric snippets from your cutting mats: Keep a lint remover near your cutting mat to pick up threads, lint, and snippets of fabric. Works like a charm. A lint remover is also handy to remove threads and lint from your clothes after sewing.

Gold Coast Quilters Guild

To print on freezer paper using an ink-jet printer, cut the freezer paper into 8½ by 11-inch pieces and press the shiny side onto regular printer paper. It feeds right through the printer. Just make sure you feed it through so the correct side will get printed. After printing, remove the regular printer paper from the freezer paper.

Doll blankets made from recycled practice squares:
I love to make quilts for dolls and stuffed animals by taking the practice quilt sandwiches I make for each project and simply even the edges and add a binding.

....

Like many quilters, I like to limber up before quilting on a finished top, and I want to try out different design ideas on the actual fabric I'm using in a project. Typically, I make a practice square that is roughly 16 by 16 inches or 20 by 20, cut out batting and backing fabric to match, and safety pin the layers together. Then I can practice on my machine, adjust the tension, try out thread and stitch ideas, and decide whether to do echo quilting or make up a pattern based on the fabric.

Fig. 11

My stepdaughter's 3-year-old, Lucy, couldn't care less if the quilting stitches are uneven or I've used four different colors of thread; it all just makes it more interesting if there is a jumble of jagged and swirly shapes and whatever else I doodled. Since I love to write words in my quilts anyway and know these are eventually going to Lucy, I sometimes write her name on the edge when I'm done with my practice quilting (Fig. 11). In one case, I made a doll quilt out of the same Olivia the Pig fabric I had used in a quilt for Lucy, so her doll has a quilt very much like hers. She loves it!

Meg Cox, President
Alliance for American Quilts
allianceforamericanquilts.com

When making a sampler quilt with every block different, make your templates from freezer paper. Iron the freezer paper template to your fabric. If you did not add the seam allowance to your template, you can use the edges of the template as your sew line and then peel off the paper when the block is finished.

Inventory control: To keep an accurate accounting of your stash, cut a sample from each piece half a yard or larger. Staple to a 3 by 5-inch index card, add the yardage, the name of the manufacturer, the name of the fabric line and color name, where you bought it and when, and the price per yard. You can then sort them by color and store them in a recipe box. This will help you shop from your stash. And when you are shopping for coordinating fabrics, just take the proper cards along with you.

To prevent raveling and fraying: Before washing the fabric, cut a small triangle off each corner. This will also tell you which fabrics have been washed. If you're washing a piece smaller than a half yard, place it in a lingerie bag before putting in the washing machine to prevent fraying.

. . . .

Before you put wet fabric into the clothes dryer, untangle and clip all loose threads. Then give each piece a hard shake to cut down on tangling and creasing.

. . . .

Ever had your machine eat up the pieces when you begin to sew? Place a small scrap of fabric under the pressure foot as you feed your sewing under the foot.

better stitching

better stitching

A family is a patchwork of love.
—*Anonymous*

Tips for satin stitching:

1. Threads that are good for machine embroidery are good for satin stitching.

2. Your needle is important. A 90/14 needle is great for satin stitching through the sandwiched layers, but it wouldn't be good when used with a single layer of fabric and stabilizer.

3. Set your machine to zigzag or satin stitch setting and adjust your stitch width as desired. Make sure the stitch is wide enough to stitch to the inside and outside of the raw edge of your appliqué. Use the 2.5-millimeter setting most often. On finer pieces and fabrics, use a narrower stitch. The narrower your stitch, the easier it is to make

clean, tight curves. Satin stitching that is too wide is just not attractive.

4. The tighter your stitch length, the better. A tight stitch means it takes longer to go around your appliqué, but it's worth the time. Set your stitch length at 0.2 millimeter for satin stitching. Your machine may not allow you to go that tight, so shorten as much as possible.

5. Use an open-toe presser foot with a channel on the underside that allows the raised satin stitching to slide

under it as you feed the piece through the machine (Fig. 12). Guide the raw edge of your appliqué into the center mark on the foot to be sure you're encasing the entire raw edge of the fabric with your stitching.

Fig. 12

6. Stitch at a comfortable pace. Start slowly if you're a novice. As your stitching improves with practice, stitch faster. The faster you are able to stitch, the better your satin stitching will look (Fig. 13).

Fig. 13

7. Satin stitching may come undone if the beginnings and endings aren't backstitched. Pull your thread tail to the front of the presser foot at the beginning of a line of satin stitching and stitch over it for an inch or so to keep it from coming undone and to hide the end.

8. Set your machine to stop with the needle in the down position when satin stitching to make pivoting easier.

9. Stitch over the raw edge with the appliqué to the left side of the needle.

Patrick Lose
Patrick Lose Studios
patricklose.net

57

Half-square triangle unit instructions (a Quick Quarter ruler works well for this):

First, pair up the two fabrics to be used in the half-square unit. Second, mark the lighter square diagonally. This will be the cutting line. Mark again, ¼ inch on each side of the first line. These will be the stitching lines (Fig. 14).

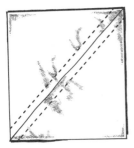

Layer a marked square with the coordinate square. Stitch on the stitching lines and cut on the cutting lines. Repeat to yield the number of half-square triangle units needed. Mark, stitch, cut, and press yields two finished units each time.

Jacque Johnson, owner
Adel Quilting & Dry Goods Co.
adelquilting.com

Fig. 14

I keep a measuring tape attached to the table in front of my sewing machine. When at class, I have a ruler there. Every time I sew pieces together, I know what size the end result should be, and I measure as soon as I sew. If it is not the correct size, I rip and resew immediately. I tell my students it is not the size of the seam that matters (although you do not want to be under an eighth of an inch, in my opinion) but the end result.

It is worth the time it takes to correct a mistake in a quilt, even if the entire top is done. Your quilt will be around a lot longer (years and years, we hope) than the time it takes to correct it.

. . . .

Snip your threads close to the seam right as you take the pieces from the machine. It will take less time than snipping them from the entire back of a quilt.

. . . .

I always make my half-square triangle units (bias squares) and quarter-square triangle units slightly bigger so I can true them perfectly to the right size and squareness.

Sharon Rehrig
Teacher and Retreats
Timely Stitches
timelystitches@rcn.com

. . . .

My longarm quilting tip is to always practice with a purpose. Learn one design and practice it until you are comfortable, then move on to something a little more challenging.

Pam Clarke
Home Stitches/Lines with Designs
homestitches.com

Machine quilting with nylon or invisible thread: When machine quilting with nylon or invisible thread, it is hard to locate the end of the thread. When you clip it off, tape it to the front left of your sewing machine with a piece of blue tape.

Gold Coast Quilters Guild

To untangle knots in your stitching, place your needle through the loop and pull it up. Then put the needle under the knot and pull up until the knot is released (Fig. 15). Pull the thread taut and continue with your stitching.

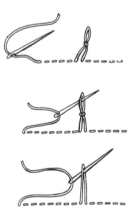

Fig. 15

When free motion quilting, always start your sewing machine sewing before you move your fabric, and always stop moving your fabric before you stop your sewing machine. This way, you will not break your needle, and you will have tie on and tie off for your threads.

Gold Coast Quilters Guild

....

When sewing bias and straight grain pieces of fabric together on the sewing machine, always put the straight grain fabric on the bottom. This helps to stabilize the bias piece.

....

To make a secure knot at the end of a line of stitching, make your last stitch, leaving a loop. Pass the needle through the loop, and you'll be making a second loop. Pass the needle through that loop, too (Fig. 16). Pull the thread snugly, and you have made a double loop.

Fig. 16

Making half-square triangles: When making two squares into half-square triangles, put two squares right sides together. Mark diagonally down the middle of one square and then sew ¼ inch on each side of the drawn line. Instead of making the base squares ⅞ inch larger than the finished square, as most patterns call for, make the base squares 1 inch larger than the finished square. This will result in trimming the two half-square triangles, but your block will never be too small.

Gold Coast Quilters Guild

Do you suffer from wandering foot pedal as you sew? To stop it, just put more of your foot on the pedal. The weight of your heel resting on the pedal instead of on the floor will keep you from pushing the pedal away as you sew.

When making half-square triangles, instead of marking everything, take the square to the ironing board, iron the mark in, then sew a scant ¼-inch seam to make two half-square triangles.

Beverly Martine
Quilt N Bee
quiltnbee.biz

Sometimes we have to rip out stitches. Use your seam ripper to cut every third stitch or so, then cover this cut line with masking tape. Flip the seam over and pull out the long thread. Flip over again and remove the masking tape. All the cut threads will stick to it. No picking!

. . . .

To achieve a perfect ¼-inch seam allowance, cut a strip of Dr. Scholl's moleskin and lay it ¼ inch away from your needle on the bed of your machine. It has an adhesive back. Dr. Scholl's moleskin is available from most pharmacies, and a package will last you a lifetime.

Gold Coast Quilters Guild

. . . .

Sewing strips or attaching borders: When sewing together strips or attaching borders, make sure you see a glimmer of the bottom fabric at the cut edge to ensure getting both layers sewn together properly. The bottom layer sometimes shifts, even when pinned.

Gold Coast Quilters Guild

patchwork piecing tips

piecing tips

patchwork piecing tips

In the crazy quilt of life, I'm glad you're in my block of friends.
—Anonymous

Test blocks: When you're trying out a block design, always use the same theme fabrics (e.g., '30s, Civil War, Halloween). This way, you will soon have enough blocks to put together a quilt.

Gold Coast Quilters Guild

Save time, thread, and energy by chain piecing. Feed the

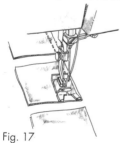

patches to be joined together through the machine, one right after the other, without ever lifting the pressure foot (Fig. 17). Leave just enough room separating each pair so they can be cut apart later as needed.

Fig. 17

Arrange and rearrange patches on a large piece of freezer paper, shiny side up. When you're pleased with the arrangement, iron them in place. You can then peel them off as you are ready to sew.

Before cutting up all that perfect fabric for the perfect quilt, cut and sew one block only. If there is a problem with the directions or seam sizes, you can fix it before have a stack of useless cut fabrics.

Gold Coast Quilters Guild

Before completing blocks, experiment with the units. Put them on a design wall. Rotate them. Add other units. Be creative (Fig. 18). In the end, you may come up with a completely different design and a simpler way to piece the quilt.

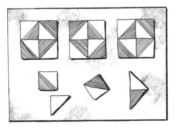

Fig. 18

Keep patches organized: One way is to clip patches together with a spring-action clothespin. Another way to keep them together is to run a long thread through the stack and back up to the top and tie into a bow knot. To store or take a larger piece to a class, fold with the raw edges to the inside and place over a hanger (Fig. 19).

Fig. 19

Heart blocks in advance: Sit down for a couple of hours every few months and make up some heart blocks. Then, when you need them, you will have them ready to go. Please send them to everyone, not just your friends. Everyone needs to know that someone is thinking about them.

Gold Coast Quilters Guild

For accurate piecing, it is of paramount importance that you sew an accurate ¼-inch seam allowance. Many sewing machines come equipped with a presser foot that measures ¼ inch from the stitching line to the right edge of the foot (Fig. 20). Test your machine by sewing a sample and measuring the seam allowance. If it is not ¼ inch, place a piece of masking tape on your machine to mark the ¼-inch seam allowance (Fig. 21).

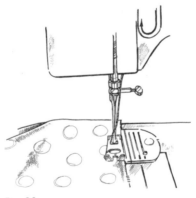

Fig. 20

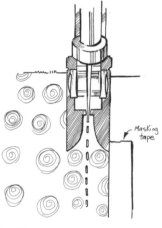

Fig. 21

When you have a variety of different shapes and pieces to piece together following a layout, place a small sticky note with the appropriate position on each piece. It will make identifying them later much easier and faster.

When cutting out pieces that have been traced around a template, cut slightly inside the marked line (Fig. 22). Hold the fabric in your left hand and cut away the marked template

71

with your right (reverse if you're left handed). The size of your cut-out piece will be more accurate.

Fig. 22

Before starting a piecing project, fill several bobbins in advance so you don't have to stop to fill a new one in the middle of sewing. Just pop in another pre-filled bobbin and you're set to go.

Use the same color thread in your bobbins when starting a piecing project. Use a light neutral such as gray or beige if you're sewing lighter fabrics and a darker shade of these colors if sewing dark fabrics. This saves a lot of bobbin changing time when sewing.

Clip finished blocks to a skirt hanger to keep them wrinkle free and out of the way (Fig. 23).

Fig. 23

appliqué tricks

appliqué tricks

Our lives are like quilts: bits and pieces,
joy and sorrow, stitched with love.
—Anonymous

In needleturn appliqué, always finger-press the turn-under allowance of your appliqué pieces before you pin them to your block. The turn-under allowance will turn under much more easily along this finger-pressed crease. This one step makes needleturning easier and faster (Fig. 24).

Fig. 24

Becky Goldsmith
Linda Jenkins
Piece O' Cake Designs
pieceocake.com

When I machine appliqué, I don't like my zigzag stitches to be too close, like a tight satin stitch. If you give a little, it is more forgiving. You won't see your errors or where you didn't go around a curve smoothly enough.

When I'm choosing thread for my zigzag stitches for machine appliqué and there are many colors in a fabric, I like to go with the darkest shade for better coverage. For example, if the ground is brown, and the elements in the print are fuchsia, white, and the like, I'm likely to choose a color that coordinates with the brown for my zigzag stitching.

Linda Lum DeBono
Lindalumdebono.com

I cut out the center of my fusible web for large shapes to reduce bulk. Please change your needles often!

Linda Lum DeBono
lindalumdebono.com

Looking for appliqué design ideas? Children's coloring books are a great source of inspiration. Many of the designs are drawn simply and are easily adapted to fabric.

Appliquéing tiny pieces? Just keep your seam allowances larger and trim as you go. That way, you have plenty of fabric to hang onto. And remember, a wooden toothpick and a little fabric glue is your friend for turning under errant threads.

Toby Preston
Kindred Quilts: A Gathering Place
kindredquilts.com

You don't know half the joy of needlework until you create something that is yours alone. Appliqué allows you the freedom to make any design. Wherever you look you see shapes and colors. Take what you want and use it in your design.

When you are using fusible web: An X-ACTO knife with a #11 blade is great for cutting out the inside of pieces such as letters.

When tracing patterns with a pencil on fusible web, the key is to press hard enough so your patterns will show up when you fuse them on dark fabric. If you press too hard you'll get graphite all over your hands and your fabric.

Once I am through fusing my shape on my appliqué sheet, I let the shape cool and then move it to a piece of wax paper.

I don't ever heat on the wax paper. It just stores the shape nice and clean so I can use the appliqué sheet again for the next shape. Once I have finished fusing I can move my shapes around on different backgrounds to see if they will work color-wise because they are neatly placed on the wax paper.

Amy Bradley
Amy Bradley Designs
amybradleydesigns.com

paper piecing is easy

paper piecing

paper piecing is easy

A bed without a quilt is like a sky without stars.
—*Anonymous*

Jodie is well known for her books and seminars on paper piecing. For some people, paper piecing is daunting. Jodie has developed these tricks and guidelines to make this fun technique fast and easy.

Paper piecing tricks:

A shortened stitch length will make the job of removing the paper from your blocks easier, thanks to the perforations added by the needle going into the paper more often.

Use a press cloth when pressing on the printed side of the pattern because the printer ink could transfer to your iron.

Color-code or mark your patterns so you stitch the correct fabric in the proper place in your block. When making multiple blocks, make an extra copy of the pattern, color code

it, and use it as a key so you can easily see where the different fabrics go (Fig. 25).

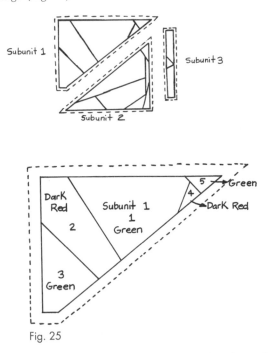

Fig. 25

Leave the paper foundation in place until after the quilt top is completed. Subunits and blocks are easier to align this way and will not become distorted by the tearing process. Don't worry about the grain line of the fabrics in your blocks. One of the beauties of foundation piecing is that the foundation stabilizes the fabrics, and as a result, it is unnecessary to follow grain line rules strictly when cutting fabric.

Things to remember:

Paper piecing is exceedingly precise and requires no precutting, so it is fast. But some sewers find it difficult to grasp because it is so unlike the way we are accustomed to sewing. These steps will help you automatically remember how to place fabric so your results are perfect every time.

1. The unprinted side of the paper is the right side of the finished block.

2. Cut the fabric for your patches larger than you think they need to be (Fig. 26). Once you develop an eye for how much you need, you can be more economical with your fabric. Especially when learning, it is better to waste fabric than have to resort to the dreaded seam ripper.

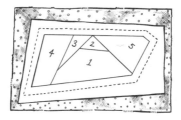

Fig. 26

85

3. Just as in regular piecing, you are always sewing with fabrics right sides together. Nothing is different other than a piece of paper on top of the fabrics, and you'll be sewing on a line on the paper.

4. Place the fabric for the next patch right side up on the bed of the sewing machine.

5. Place the paper/block printed side up over the fabric you just laid down. Have the patch with the lower number, the one you just sewed, pointing to your left, and the patch you are adding will be to your right. Don't think about this; just do it. The bulk of the fabric (that you will fold back to cover the space on the paper) will be extending to your left.

6. The printed side of your pattern will be the wrong side of the finished block. You will be sewing with the printed side of the block facing up so you can see the lines. Your fabric will be underneath the paper, on the right side of the block.

7. No one is going to see your seam allowances, so don't bother making them perfect.

Jodie has also developed a unique technique for curved paper piecing. This not only makes the task of sewing curves easy and quick but also adds the plus of texture to the surface. Go to her Web site at jodieandcompany.com for a full instructional video for curved paper piecing. You can also learn Jodie's paper piecing techniques on the Web site.

marking and quilting the top

marking

marking and quilting the top

I keep my end tables full of quilting so I don't have to dust them.

—*Anonymous*

When removing water-soluble blue marking pen lines, use an ice cube. Just run an ice cube across the blue mark. No getting the quilt project soaking wet with spray or washcloth. Target only the area that is blue.

> Linda Mather
> *Tomorrow's Quilts*
> tomorrowsquilts.com

Marking a quilt for quilting: One of the best ways to mark a quilt for quilting is with Crayola White Chalk. It must be Crayola. Sharpen it with a crayon sharpener. It goes on easily and brushes off easily. This will work only if you do a section at a time. Do not use the colored chalk.

> *Gold Coast Quilters Guild*

When I first learned to quilt, my quilt mentor (also named Jane) taught me to use slivers of bath soap for marking. There would have been very few, if any, marking products on the market at that time, in the 1960s. I still think soap shards are excellent for marking around templates or for marking quilting patterns. They may be considered green in today's quilting world!

Jane Quinn
Quilting in the Country
QuiltingInTheCountry.com

A mechanical pencil with its thin, hard lead works well in marking thin lines on light-colored fabrics. Also, it never has to be sharpened.

Easy way to make quilt sandwich: If you have table pads for your dining room table, use them when you assemble your quilt for quilting. Put all the leaves in your table and place the table pads on the table felt side up. Then put all the layers in place without all the normal slipping and sliding. The "sandwich" will stay put while you pin baste or hand baste the layers together.

Marilyn Steen
Sun Lakes, Arizona

Thread an entire pack of needles onto one spool of thread (Fig. 27). When you're ready to quilt, pull the desired

length of thread with the first needle (hold the other needles back), tuck the thread into the cut at the top of the spool, and cut the thread. You're good to go, and you won't have to stop to thread the needle each time you need additional thread.

Fig. 27

In machine quilting, the design should be a continuous line. It takes some forethought deciding where to start and stop before sewing. Use a large pad of paper to rehearse. Transfer the quilting motif and trace the design with a pencil again and again. Then go to the machine to stitch.

Quilting patterns are simple regardless of their size or whether they are hand or machine stitched. The pattern isn't quilted, it is the background. You're working with light. To contrast with shadows, the light must lie on a smooth surface. The pattern stands out in bas-relief because the light on it is unbroken. The quilting, with its hills and valleys, puts the quilted fabric in shadow.

Pinning your quilt before quilting: You don't need to buy a special tool to close your safety pins before quilting. Use a grapefruit spoon that has ridges to close all of the pins. This will really save your fingertips.

Gold Coast Quilters Guild

. . . .

When I'm machine quilting, I listen to music on my iPod to keep me energized and in the zone. I always try to choose the appropriate music to match my quilting designs.

Elin Waterston
elinwaterston.com

. . . .

When basting your quilt top, stitch into an old spoon. Thread an embroidery or crewel needle and place the quilt on a hard surface. Place the spoon in your left hand (reverse if you're left handed) and push the quilt down just in front of the needle (Fig. 28). As the tip of the needle hits the spoon it will glide up the bowl, where you can easily grip the needle and pull the thread through.

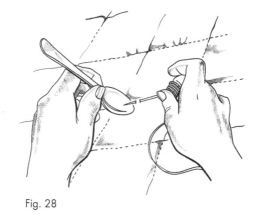

Fig. 28

I use monofilament thread to quilt a lot because I use so many different colors in my quilt. Sometimes the tension is off and my thread breaks. Instead of loading the spool on the holder on my machine, I place the spool in a baby food jar, put it beside my machine, and adjust to get the right tension.

Jenice Belling
The Quilted Garden and
Quilted Garden Designs
quiltedgarden.com

It's really annoying when spools of thread start unwinding on their own. Here's an easy way to put a stop to it. Unwind 6

inches of thread. Wrap the thread around the spool one time, catching your finger under the thread. Thread the end under the loop made by your finger (Fig. 29), remove your finger, and pull taut. You've created a slip knot. The thread can still be pulled off the spool, but it will not unwind on its own.

Fig. 29

binding perfection

binding

binding perfection

Quilters know all the angles.
—*Anonymous*

To create a continuous bias binding strip:

1. Cut the fabric square in half diagonally. Place the two triangle pieces right sides together with the straight edges on the right (Fig. 30). Press seam open.

2. Using a transparent gridded ruler, draw a parallel line every 2¼ inches (or width needed) on the wrong side of the fabric (Fig. 31).

3. Fold the marked piece right sides together to form a tube, aligning the edges and pinning the marked lines so one width of the binding extends beyond the edge on each side as shown (Fig. 32). Sew the tube together with a ¼-inch seam. Press the seam open. Cut on the marked line to make one continuous 2¼-inch-wide bias binding strip.

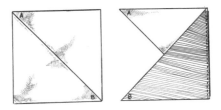

Fig. 30

Fig. 31   Fig. 32

Patrick Lose
Patrick Lose Studios
patricklose.net

When binding a quilt for a baby, bind it with a cotton binding before using the silky baby binding. That way, when the silky binding wears thin or the child outgrows the silky binding, your quilt is still bound with regular cotton underneath.

Maribeth and Jackie
The Calico Cow Quilt Shop
thecalicocow.com

Leftover bindings: Keep all your leftover pieces of bindings and sew them together to make colorful bindings for a scrappy quilt.

Gold Coast Quilters Guild

Securing binding before stitching: Rather than using straight pins to secure the binding in position for blind stitching around a quilt, use the little curved clips that look like barrette clips. They snap on and off quickly and don't have sharp points that prick you, and they are easily adjusted.

Gold Coast Quilters Guild

When making a hanging sleeve, fold the raw edges together and baste the sleeve to the top edge of the quilt. After the binding is stitched in place, hand sew the bottom edge of the sleeve to the backing.

After you make your quilt and it's ready to be quilted, make the binding, put it in a plastic baggie, and mark which quilt it belongs to or pin the baggie to the quilt. This way, you will have the binding ready when the quilting is finished.

Gold Coast Quilters Guild

....

Be careful not to stretch bias binding as you apply it to your project. If stretched, your project will saucer, which isn't the look you want.

Patrick Lose
Patrick Lose Studios
Patricklose.net

....

To apply straight grain binding, begin at the center of one side.

1. Start stitching 6 inches from the beginning of the binding strip using a ¼-inch seam allowance (Fig. 33).

2. Sew through all layers, stopping ¼ inch from the corner (Fig. 34). Backstitch, clip threads, and remove from the sewing machine. Fold the binding up (Fig. 35).

3. Fold the binding back down, aligning with the top edge and the next edge to be stitched (Fig. 36). Continue stitching around the quilt, repeating steps 2 and 3 to turn each corner.

4. Stop stitching 8 inches from where you started. Fold the binding back on itself (be sure to smooth out any slack) and butt the fold up to the beginning of the binding strip (Fig. 37).

5. Mark the binding to the left of the fold using the measurement for the total width of the binding (Fig. 38). Cut away the binding beyond the marked line.

6. Open up the binding and place the two ends right sides together at a right angle. The wrong side of the beginning end of the binding should face up (Fig. 39). Pin the strips together and mark a stitching line corner to corner. Stitch, making a mitered seam. Trim and press open. Refold the binding and finish machine stitching binding to the quilt.

7. Turn binding to the back side and pin or clip in place. At the corners neatly fold a miter (Fig. 40). Sew the binding in place by hand.

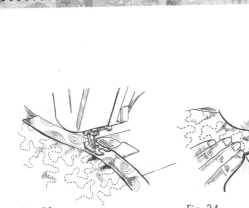

Fig. 33

Fig. 34

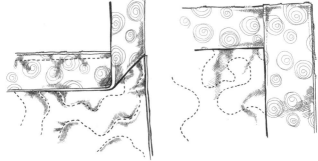

Fig. 35

Fig. 36

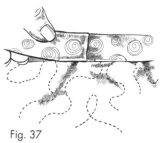

Fig. 37

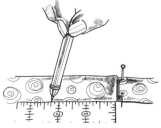

Fig. 38

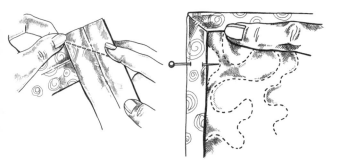

Fig. 39

Fig. 40

Miniature quilts can be hung without a hanging sleeve. Insert two safety pins vertically into the quilt backing at the upper corners. Point the circle ends of the pins toward the top. Tap two nails into the wall and slip the safety pin circles over the nail heads.

....

Pressing bindings: When pressing bindings for a quilt, secure the raw edges together with a straight pin on your ironing board. This way, you get a straight edge.

Gold Coast Quilters Guild

labeling and documenting your quilt

labeling and documenting your quilt

Finished is way better than perfect.
—Anonymous

When making a label on the back of a child's quilt, make it a pocket and put in a secret letter. It's also fun to quilt little sayings and phrases into a quilt using glow-in-the-dark thread. I have embroidered names onto kids' pillowcases with this thread. When they went to bed and turned out the lights, they were really surprised.

. . . .

I make donation quilts and use old jeans pockets. I sandwich batting between two 36 by 36-inch pieces of fabrics

and quilt them together. Then I sew the jeans pocket on and place a little teddy bear in the pocket (Fig. 41). Children love snuggling with their quilt and their teddy bear all at once.

Fig. 41

Here's a simple way to attach a label. Design your label with a ½-inch border all around. Cut a piece of fusible the size of the label without the border and attach to the label. Fuse the label in place on the quilt. Turn under the raw edge ¼ inch and hand stitch in place.

Linda Freyer
Coral Springs, Florida

Document your quilts: Before you give your quilt away or keep for your own use, document it with a few pictures (a full-size one and several detail pictures, including the back and the label). You can collect all your pictures in a three-ring binder along with the patterns, fabric swatches, and any other information you want to remember. It's so gratifying to look back on your work when the information is located all in one place. Also, you can take your book to quilt camp or bee for show & tell, even when you no longer have the quilts.

Gold Coast Quilters Guild

Documenting your quilts: The mission of the Alliance for American Quilts is to preserve and share the stories of quilts and their makers, and I've become an even stronger advocate of documenting quilts. I've had the experience of inheriting family quilts and knowing nothing about the story behind the quilt and its maker, and it drives me nuts because all the people who could answer my questions have passed away. When we make a quilt for a loved one, we are confident that person will treasure the quilt and remember where it came from, but will their children and grandchildren know? They probably won't have a clue.

....

The basics:

At the very least, make sure that your quilt labels include the following:

- Your full name (maiden and married, if that applies)
- Date the quilt was finished
- Place the quilt was made
- Recipient of the quilt (and mention of a special occasion such as birthday or anniversary)

Optional extras, much appreciated by descendants, collectors, and curators:

- State whether the design was original. If not, credit the designer.
- State whether the quilting was done by you or another.
- Care instructions are very helpful.

If this is a masterpiece quilt with a special family story behind it, please consider going further. Write a letter about the quilt and keep it with the quilt. One way to do this is to create a simple fabric pocket for the quilt back and place the paper inside the pocket. If the quilt is used on a bed, the crinkly paper can be put aside, but try to tuck it back into the fabric envelope when the quilt is put away in storage.

Meg Cox, president
Alliance for American Quilts
allianceforamericanquilts.com

sewing machine
maintenance

sewing machine maintenance

Quilt 'til you wilt.
—*Anonymous*

Here are a few things that everyone can and should do for their sewing machine on a regular basis. Please keep in mind that every sewing machine should see a professional for a full service every few years. Just to be clear, a few years is two or three; five years is half a decade, and way too long between professional services. Also, the older the machine, the more regularly you should use it. Machine oil and lubricant (white grease) will dry up if the working parts of the machines are not put to use. Even if you do not have a project to work on, it is a good idea to run your machine at least five minutes per month. This may be done without thread, needle, or bobbin. You simply need to keep the lubricants moving through the machine.

Here are a few things you may do often:

1. Use good-quality thread and needles.

2. Change your needle after every few hours of use, and try to use the proper needle for the job. A wide variety of needle choices are available, and your dealer will be happy to educate you on the different reasons to pick different needles.

3. Oil your hook. The hook is the part of the machine that rotates around the bobbin and bobbin case. The hook picks up the thread from behind the needle's eye and wraps it around your bobbin. You should dust out the lint from around the hook, remove the bobbin, and drop one or two drops of oil in the part of the hook that moves around the basket (the part that holds the bobbin and bobbin case). This should be done after you have used about five bobbins of thread. If you're on a sewing marathon, once a day is enough.

4. Clean your feed dogs. Your sewing machine was not manufactured with little felt pads between the feed dogs, that is, the lint from hours of sewing fun (Fig. 42). You should remove your needle and presser foot, and then remove your stitch plate. Most stitch plates with lift up with a slight pressure from between the machine body and the plate itself. Many older machines have one or two flathead screws that hold the plate down from the top. Use a very short-handled screwdriver to loosen these

screws. My favorite mini-screwdriver has little wings on the handle so that I can apply a good amount of pressure even on a small handle (Fig. 43). Once the plate is off, dust out the space between the feed dogs. If the feed dogs are teeth, then you are flossing the gums of the feed dogs. The more lint, the less lift on the feed system, the poorer the quality of your stitch.

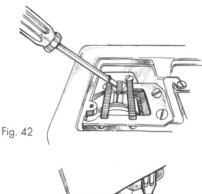

Fig. 42

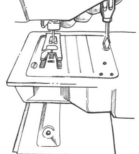

Fig. 43

5. Last, but most important, never use cans of "spray air" or "air duster." These products are CO_2 propelled and will blast moisture into your machine and make mud out of the lint you were trying to remove. It's best to use a nylon brush for all your cleanings. You may use an air compressor if it has a moisture trap on it, but you should remove the stitch plate and blow down and out through that opening. Your sewing machine mechanic will remove all the exterior covers before he blasts the machine with compressed air. You do not want to pack lint back into the machine.

A few tests you should know how to perform:

1. **Timing:** To confirm that your machine is in the proper timing for the needle and hook relationship, insert a new needle and thread the machine, lower your tension a bit, and run your very widest zigzag stitch. If the stitch forms on both sides, then your machine is well timed.

2. **What's that ticking noise?** If you are concerned that you are hearing a ticking noise in your machine, remove the bobbin and bobbin case and the thread. Insert a new needle and run the machine with the presser foot in a position so that the feed dogs are not hitting the bottom of the presser foot (that would make a terrible noise) and listen for the tick. If no tick, then try it in your widest zigzag; if still no tick, then thread the machine and

replace the bobbin and bobbin case. If the tick returns, you know that it is simply the sound of the thread coming off the position finger and that you do not need to be concerned.

3. **Thread tension:** The most common mistake made in troubleshooting your thread tension is when you find big loops of thread on the underside of the fabric. Everyone blames the bobbin at first, but it is rarely the fault of the bobbin at all (Fig. 44). If you get big loops, ½ to 1 inch long, then it is most often caused by the thread's not being in the upper tension correctly. Here is the key: The lifting of the presser foot opens the tension assembly on most home sewing machines. In other words, you must thread the machine with the presser foot in the highest resting position. The tension discs will be wide open to accept your thread. Often people leave the foot down to prevent the fabric from slipping out of location as they rethread the machine. The needle must be up to thread, so we put the foot down. Oh no. The thread will not be under tension, make a bunch of noise and a big mess under the fabric. Now you are frustrated, so you lift the foot, pull the fabric out to clear the jam, and the next time you stitch, the tension is perfect. Baffled? Perhaps the tugging in frustration allowed the thread to get where it needed to be, and now you are ready to sew.

Fig. 44

Little loops, like specks on the bottom, simply mean you need to tighten the top tension or loosen the bobbin. For speckling on the top, just loosen the top tension. If you are still getting irregular speckling, change your needle and match your threads; nobody is perfect.

Just remember that you will become very familiar with your sewing machine, and you can care for it on a regular basis. Do not forget to have a full service done every few years by a professional, and make sure you get a detailed list of the work performed by the technician who cared for your machine.

Rob Appell
Rob Appell Designs
robappell.com

we all could use some
inspiration

we all could use some inspiration

Blankets wrap you in warmth,
quilts wrap you in love.
—*Anonymous*

Ideally, you should be able to get a little distance from your design wall to view it. Place it on a wall opposite where you cut or sew. Is there no place for a design wall? Buy a portable one, or do as I did and make one from PVC pipes and fittings, fabric, and cotton batting. Until then, use the floor at the bottom of a stairway. Walk upstairs and enjoy the view. You will get some exercise, too, as you make changes and view again.

....

Use your digital camera to record what you see. Save the photos in various folders: border ideas, blocks, settings, and so on. Then, when deciding upon the final layout of a quilt or when looking for inspiration for a new quilt, review your photos.

Debbie Caffrey
debbiescreativemoments.com

Let your imagination be your inspiration!

Dream. Create. Inspire.

Ann Kisro and Susan Kisro
The Quilting Cupboard, LLC
The QC Designs
thequiltingcupboard.com

I am always fascinated by the way basic squares, circles, and triangles can become the simple building blocks in designs of great richness and ingenuity. Even basic square patches all the same size can be used to create complex compositions. For example, just setting square patches on point, so they look like fat diamonds, will give a quilt a totally different look than one in which the squares are presented in their standard orientation. And if the pattern and color in one square reach out to relate to its neighbor, the square can become downright camouflaged, making the design even more intriguing.

Kaffe Fassett
Kaffe Fassett Design
kaffefassett.com

Look more closely at the world around you for inspiration in both color and shape. Add striking hues to simple shapes, and you're sure to come up with your own original, spectacular quilts.

Kaffe Fassett
Kaffe Fassett Design
kaffefassett.com

Look and learn: Look at finished quilts at your local quilt shop. Look at quilt books and magazines. If there's a quilt show within 50 miles of you, grab a friend and make a day of it. Plan to go to International Quilt Festival, held in Houston each fall, at least once in your lifetime. Go to quilts.com for information on this show and their regional festivals.

Visit the Alliance for American Quilts online at allianceforamericanquilts.com for photos and information on more than fifty thousand quilts. The Alliance for American Quilts is a nonprofit organization whose mission is to document, preserve, and share our American quilt heritage by collecting the rich stories that historic and contemporary quilts, and their makers, tell about our nation's diverse peoples and their communities.

Quilts matter! They tell stories and illuminate our history. They link generations and foster community. They are one of the most universally recognized American art forms. Today 27 million Americans are involved in quilt making.

· ·

I just put pieces together 'til they sing; if not, I try some other combination.

> *Kaffe Fassett*
> *Kaffe Fassett Studio*
> kaffefassett.com

· ·

Start your own quilting library: Begin with Barbara Brackman's *Encyclopedia of Pieced Quilt Pattern* or Jenny Beyer's *The Quilter's Album of Patchwork Patterns.* Also, add *Encyclopedia of Applique* by Brackman. For a wonderful read, try to find a copy of *Book of American Needlework* by Rose Wilder Lane. Look through your local library's collection of quilting books, visit your local bookstore, and review the books available at your local quilt shop. Check out the books available at Amazon; you'll be amazed.

Be sure to start a subscription (if you don't already have one) to a quilting magazine such as Fons and Porter's *Love of Quilting* or *Quilter's Newsletter*. Many more are available, including ones specializing in art quilting. In addition, electronic editions of some magazines are available today. Isn't our electronic age wonderful?

Use the Internet: If you're not computer savvy, it's time to learn. There is so much available at our fingertips. Do you know about QNNtv.com? It's an online television network offering on-demand quilting videos 24 hours a day, including quilting shows produced for traditional television and two monthly series (with more on the way) produced just for QNNtv.com. The QNNtv.com library includes more than one thousand shows ready for viewing. Another online opportunity is *The Quilt Show*, offering a new show each month.

If you haven't Googled quilting yet, give it a try. You'll be amazed at the information that's just a click away. Quilting communities abound on the Internet. Go to quilting.about.com as an example.

Every fabric company providing fabrics for quilting has a Web site where you can preview its fabric lines. See the back of this book for a list of companies and their Web addresses. Many offer free patterns or show quilts using their fabrics.

If you have no nearby quilt shop, do not fret. There are countless online quilt shops just waiting for you to browse and shop.

fabric companies
and their web sites

fabric companies and their web sites

*Good friends are like quilts: They age
with you but never lose their warmth.*
—Anonymous

A. E. Nathan Co., Inc.
aenathan.com

**Alexander Henry
Fabrics, Inc.**
ahfabrics.com

Andover Fabrics
andoverfabrics.com

**Bali Fabrics and Princess
Mirah Designs**
bali-fabrics.com

Batik Textiles
batiktextiles.com

Benartex, Inc.
benartex.com

Blank Quilting
blankquilting.com

Clothworks Textiles
clothworkstextiles.com

David Textiles, Inc.
davidtextilesinc.com

Exclusively Quilters
classiccottons.com

Fabri-Quilt, Inc.
fabri-quilt.com

Free Spirit Fabric
Freespiritfabric.com

Henry Glass & Co.
henryglassfabrics.com

Hoffman California Fabrics
hoffmanfabrics.com

In the Beginning Fabrics
inthebeginningfabrics.com

Indonesian Batiks
indobatiks.com

Island Batik Inc.
islandbatik.com

James Thompson & Co. Inc.
jamesthompson.com

Kona Bay Fabrics
konabay.com

LakeHouse Dry Goods
lakehousedrygoods.com

Marcus Brothers Textiles
marcusbrothers.com

Michael Miller Fabrics
michaelmillerfabrics.com

Moda Fabrics
modafabrics.com

Northcott Fabrics
northcott.net

P & B Textiles
pbtex.com

Quilting Treasures
quiltingtreasures.com

Red Rooster Fabrics
redroosterfabrics.com

RJR Fabrics
rjrfabrics.com

Robert Kaufman Fabrics
robertkaufman.com

Troy Corp.
Troy-Corp.com

Westminster Fibers, Inc.
westminsterfibers.com

Wilmington Prints
wilmingtonprints.com

Windham Fabrics
windhamfabrics.com

COLLECT ALL
POCKET POSH® TITLES!